# No tatt before you're thirty

## What I'll tell my children . . .

Sam de Brito

PENGUIN BOOKS

# What I'll tell my children …

Ever been given a particularly resonant piece of advice, sat back and thought, 'Happy days, why didn't somebody tell me that ten years ago?' Like, you have to remove the poo tube from prawns, learn a second language before your brain starts to shrink from alcohol and caffeine, and never play poker with a guy who has the same name as an American city.

Growing up, I got a few pearls from my parents, but they were usually about what *not* to do and never the important stuff like how to bed a princess, wangle a pay rise or beat some boxhead bully in a schoolyard brawl. As I got older, the gems of hard-won experience started to accrue, but not being in a meaningful relationship, let alone blessed with children, I had no-one to pass my sometimes questionable wisdom on to.

Watching friends with their kids, I realised that they, through no motive other than love, tended to sugar-coat life's harsh realities for their offspring. Like a Hollywood romantic comedy, their advice was theoretically solid but lacked the ring of truth.

Maybe I could help?

As a blogger for the *Age* and *Sydney Morning Herald*, and a scriptwriter for some of the country's most popular TV shows, including *Water Rats*, *White Collar Blue* and *Stingers*, it's been my job to uncover and dramatise the quiet truths of human nature – the stuff we nod our heads about and say, 'That is sooo true.'

You won't find a singsong entry in this book that says, 'Magic happens' or 'Climb a tree with a child'. There are no pictures of cuddly animals. The advice is not what you'll hear from your local priest or the headmistress at a snooty girls' school. It's the stuff I wish somebody, *anybody*, had told me twenty years ago.

To avoid repetition, the items are listed once, by sex, with almost all of them applicable to boys and girls, so please don't think I'm being sexist when I warn my daughter about the dangers of video cameras and panel vans and my son about the lunacy of jogging in Speedos.

What follows may be deemed inappropriate by some readers, but there's no denying its veracity. For better or worse, this is what I've learned from my time on the planet and it's what I'll be telling both my daughter and my son . . . when I get around to having children.

Enjoy.

To my
gorgeous daughter . . .

# All men are liars

Any male between the age of thirteen and death who says, 'I just want to be friends,' wants to sleep with you. Men will say anything to get you in bed and none of them are to be trusted.

# Get a law degree

If you want to be an actor, go for it, but you might as well do paralegal work on the side rather than wait tables. Lawyers understand the levers that move the world – fear and desire – much like strippers do. And while both get paid by the hour, lawyers don't have to lap dance.

# Don't take it personally

Nine times out of ten, the seemingly inexcusable things people do and say are the result of the psycho-drama in their head. You probably remind them of the girl in Year 8 who laughed at the pee-dot on the front of their school pants.

# Hold your farts

This is hypocritical because your brother can pipe the national anthem out his backside (often while sitting on you), but you should never break wind in a man's presence, just like he should never moisturise in front of you. Once you've bedded and wedded him, however, all bets are off and give as good as you get.

# Never phone a man

Ever. Guys don't need encouragement. They just get cocky if they think you're too attainable. Blokes are like weeds – ignore them and they're everywhere.

However …

# Return his phone calls

Even if it's to say, 'Thanks, but no thanks.' Guys have feelings too and no-one likes being ignored.

Basic courtesy satisfies most stalkers.

# Be immaculate

I know your mother says you're made of sugar and spice and all things nice, but that stuff turns to jam on hot days. Impeccable grooming will take you more places than a Learjet.

# Let men do the chasing

This will be frustrating. 'I'm a modern woman,' you'll say. 'Surely I can shake the trees I wanna climb?' As a rule, men have less respect for women who pursue them than the ones they have to fight for. The thrill of the hunt is embedded in men's DNA – it's a law of nature. At least you don't have to worry about the size of your penis or going bald.

# Tell me if you're experimenting

Your father definitely knows more about drugs than the girls at school, so please talk to me if you're thinking of trying something and we'll map out the pitfalls. Some of the most interesting people you'll meet will have taken drugs but, remember, many of the saddest will be the ones who didn't know when to stop.

# Don't be rude to guys who talk to you

They're only doing it because they find you attractive. If you don't want to speak to them, tell them you've got a boyfriend who races Formula 1.

# Know your style

You know how pathetic it is when a guy can't kick a football? It's the same with girls and clothes. Fashion is important, so educate yourself. But remember, just because your girlfriends are dressing like Paris Hilton doesn't mean you have to. Find your own look and embrace it. Unless it's goth.

# Learn about finances

Educate yourself about the principles of investment. Make your money work for you, or you'll still be working for it when you're seventy. There's nothing cooler than a woman who trades stocks to supplement her income.

# Take lots of photos

You think you look dorky now? Trust me, you look fantastic, girl, and you'll appreciate the memories.

# Never date a guy named Miles

Or Hendrix or Jett. Any parent who names their son after a unit of measurement or a dead singer has to be pretentious. There's a good chance their kid will be as well.

# Seek a mentor in your field

Once you know what you want to do with your life, commit yourself to it 100 per cent. Find someone who's done it all and get their advice. Old people love to talk about themselves.

# Don't do drugs with strangers

If there's a chance you're gonna lose control, you want to be among friends, not some lurking date-rapey Casanova you just met on the dance floor. Friends will throw you into a cab and stay with you until the refrigerator stops speaking Urdu.

# Don't date guys who wear gold jewellery

It's like licking a power switch – why would you do it to yourself?

# Forget tanning

They might tease you at school for being pale, but you'll get your own back when the sun queens turn forty and look like the bladder from a grand final football.

# Don't date guys who ride motorbikes or drive panel vans

They're both incredibly dangerous, but for different reasons.

# Play sport

Enjoy your body and what it's capable of when you're young. Even if you're a complete unco at seventeen, you're an absolute Olympian compared to what you can do at thirty-five.

# Never have sex on the first date

He'll still be there for date two and, believe me, he'll respect you more for making him work for it. Unless, of course, he's going to war, then why not send the poor bugger off with a smile on his face?

# Drink beer

It shows you're down-to-earth, low maintenance and maybe even appreciate ball sports.

(Just like your dad.)

# Don't date professional athletes, actors or musicians

If they're successful, they'll be cheating on you.
If they're not, they'll be using bed sheets as curtains
when they're forty.

# However, if you're just interested in sex

Well, those creative types are *creative*.

And athletes are fit.

# If your boyfriend asks you to iron his shirt

Say no. Or do a *really* bad job.
He'll never ask again.

# Stand up for old people

Unless they're wearing a raincoat and seem unusually pleased to see you. If they don't thank you, the next time the bus lurches pretend to lose your balance and drop a sly elbow onto the top of their head – they'll get the message.

# Orgasms are a shared responsibility

Men can be incredibly ignorant about what pleases a woman. Be comfortable enough with your body to tell him what you need to get you across the line – it will make sex that much more fulfilling for you and your partner.

# Never have sex on camera

If you really, really, *really* feel it's something you want to do, take the tape when you leave. (But don't label it 'My Sex Video' and put it on your bookshelf.)

# Don't sleep with your flatmate

It always gets weird and never works out.

# Don't ask people what they do or where they're from

Everyone has a story to tell, so draw it out of them without preconceptions based on their address or income. Stuck for an opener? Ask their opinion on the topic of the day, rather than rushing in and giving yours.

# No tattoos before you're thirty

You can have one on your face after that, but rest assured, you won't get a dolphin leaping over your belly button if you wait till then.

# Don't send love letters

By all means write a long missive to your beau, drain your heart, map your very interior. Now put it in the bottom drawer of your desk, don't look at it for three weeks, then read it. Thank me later.

# If in doubt, go without

Which applies to clothes, one-night stands, tequila shots and takeaway food.

# Always choose the man who makes you laugh

Don't date men just for their looks, money or status. The six-pack of abdominals fades, the sense of humour doesn't.

# Don't smoke

This applies to your brother as well. It has no redeeming qualities. It stinks, gives you wrinkles, can eventually kill you . . . and you'll steal my ciggies.

# Read

Someone's taken the time to distil their thoughts on life into a few hundred pages, and it's sitting there for you to experience. You only live once, and something in that book may make your life that little bit easier.

# Have a baby when you want to

Life's changing fast. The man of your dreams may not be there forever, but your child will be. This is the most important relationship of your life – just make sure you're in the emotional and financial position to do it.

# Never be the other woman

No-one likes a home wrecker. You'll be blamed for the infidelity and he'll more than likely stay with his wife.

# Don't roll your eyes

It's rude, suggests you think you're better than other people and you look like you've just trodden barefoot on a snail.

# Don't put all your eggs in one bastard

Be independent. Have a career, wealth and social circle outside of your partner's.

# Have female friends

Don't be one of those girls who say, 'I prefer the company of men to women.' You will grow up lonely.

# Never throw a drink in a guy's face

It's not high drama. It's cheap. Walk away. On the other hand, if he's groped you, make sure the glass is nice and full.

# Take risks

I promise you won't be on your deathbed wishing you hadn't kissed that cute French boy or launched that fashion label. Do it – just check your bungee cord is secure.

# Don't talk to children in coochie-woochie baby voices

It shits me.

# Travel. Alone. Wisely.

As soon as you can. You'll meet more people by yourself and can't hide behind your friends. You'll learn about other cultures first-hand and become more open-minded. You'll also realise there's no place quite like home.

# Remember people's names

Unless it's the guy who rides the motorbike.

# Drive a cool car

It doesn't have to be expensive. For the same price as a hatchback made of tinfoil, you'll get an old-school V8 you can't dent with dynamite. After all, it's only fossil fuel.

# You *can* be too skinny

If you must focus on your body, make it positive and get addicted to fitness. Exercise becomes a habit, and it's better than eating cheesecake when you're feeling down. You'll be thankful when you're the only one of your friends who doesn't have a lovely little osteoporosis hump when you're eighty-five.

# Don't be the drunk chick

It's never attractive and sometimes downright dangerous. While we're on the subject, if you wake up more than twice in your life with someone whose name you can't remember, give up the booze forever.

# Don't use emoticons ;-)

They're just annoying.

# Don't be rude to waiters

Or cab drivers, or anyone you believe is in a position of inferiority – even when there's no-one else around.

# Never let someone humiliate you during sex

It's a crazy thing being naked with a stranger and sometimes, in the heat of the bedroom (or toilet cubicle), people ask or do something that can make you uncomfortable. The first time tell them no. If they do it again, walk away and never come back. It's your body, so don't feel pressured to act out other people's pornographic fantasies.

# Eat music

Listen to it all and give everything a chance. It can make you happier than just about anything on earth.

# Compare nothing

Be it bust size, salary or your childhood. Comparison to your own will just make you grumpy or smug.

# Don't be a groupie

Be the rock star.

# Be one of the cool chicks

Which doesn't mean the bimbo who teases the fat girl at school. It means defining your opinions beyond what your friends and parents think, having a humanity that may put you at odds with others, being able to laugh at yourself and, above all, wearing great shoes.

# Be kind

It's the most attractive quality you'll ever possess.

To my
dashing son . . .

# Become an investment banker

Everyone hates their job till their thirties when, if they're lucky, they work out what they really want to do. Here's a little secret – life's all about cash, son. Dabbling in filmmaking or designing your own range of organic yoga wear is a lot more fun after you've made 40 million dollars as a derivatives trader.

# Don't masturbate (too much)

It makes you lazy. Your penis will drag you ridiculous places trying to get you laid, even when all you want to do is blob out on the couch. The upside is you'll see a whole lot of life, which is better than being hunched over Internet porn in your bedroom.

# Learn to fight

I don't care if it's boxing or jujitsu. The rule is you never get physical until they touch you or a woman. Then you'll know how to break their jaw.

# Don't be scared

This is so important it should philosophically inform every moment of your life. Unless you're in physical danger, fear is nature's way of telling you you're about to grow.

# Learn a trade

If the life of a suit doesn't appeal, try manual labour. There's a huge shortage of skilled tradespeople looming and plumbers will soon charge more than surgeons. Do an apprenticeship, learn some computer skills and seek moderate business guidance, and you'll be absolutely loaded in twenty years.

# Have female friends

And lots of them. It teaches you to respect women, gives you insight into the feminine mind . . . and it's a great way to meet other chicks.

# Talk to her!

You know that feeling you get in your stomach before you approach a beautiful girl? That's the worst it ever gets. As soon as you actually speak to her, the cramps disappear. Do this enough times, you'll soon stop laughing nervously and saying dumb things, and eventually become 'one of those guys' who are completely at ease in the company of the opposite sex.

# Don't lie about stupid stuff

Don't bullshit people about places you've been or women you've slept with. You need to save your lies for really important occasions, such as salary negotiations and references for friends.

# If you can make a girl laugh

You can kiss her. If you can kiss her, well, you know the rest. Humour's a great weapon. If the corpses on *Saturday Night Live* can make a living being 'funny', you can bust enough one-liners to score a date.

# Don't trust florists

Specify the flowers, dude. They'll end up sending carnations and you'll be dead in the water.

# Get crazy haircuts

Before you go bald. Do it all, son. Mohawks, blue mullets, rat's-tails. Who cares if old ladies won't get in lifts with you? That's what youth's for.

But remember . . .

# Never get dreads

Is there a worse look on earth than a white guy with dreadlocks? Maybe the permed Asian, the blond black dude or, God help us, the toupee. If you're white, you're never gonna be Bob Marley, so live with it. And if you do go bald, shave it close – don't be that guy with the monkey's bum on his head.

# Never say 'my lady friend'

It makes you sound like you should be in a Rod Stewart music video wearing a cape.

# Respect cops

You don't have to like them, but appreciate the job they do. It's a brutal occupation, and they're the first people you call when the shit hits the fan.

# Romance an older woman

By the time you're twenty-one, you should have had a sexual relationship with a woman ten years your senior. It demystifies the process, you learn what bits really do what and discover an amazing new concept – afterglow.

# Don't be cheap

Tip waiters and don't haggle over restaurant or phone bills. People will take advantage of it, but who cares? Being labelled cheap is like being known as smelly or boring – it's hard to prove otherwise.

# Learn good manners

You can look like a god and dress like an aristocrat, but hold your knife like an icepick and it's all over in the first-impression stakes.

# Work on the mother

You'll make your life so much easier with girlfriends' parents if you can master the art of the first impression. Dress nicely, have clean fingernails and make Mum laugh. Dad will follow.

# Look people in the eye

Hold their gaze. Don't look away – it suggests weakness.
Practise it.

# Be charming

Charm is the ability to get the answer 'yes' without ever having to ask the question. When you understand this, you'll probably already be married.

# Don't worry about your penis

There's not a whole lot you can do about your spanner, so be proud of it. Give it a name – Pedro is always amusing.

# Learn a language

You can visit the most beautiful country on earth but if you can't speak to the locals, you're only experiencing half of what it has to offer. Learning a language is like putting on someone else's skin and seeing the world through their eyes. Unfortunately, the older you get, the harder it is to learn a foreign tongue, so start before your brain looks like a walnut from all those nights out with the boys.

# Don't let a woman lead you through a crowd

It just screams wuss.

# Do say, 'I'm dropping the kids off at the pool'

Or 'I'm off to build a log cabin' or 'I'm giving birth to the boss.' It's much funnier than announcing you're 'taking a dump.'

# Move slowly. Take up space. Don't fidget.

Watch any movie star and you'll see he does everything in his own time. Only forest animals and guys wearing tight underpants move too quickly.

# Never be needy

Nothing will scare women away faster than being a clinging sook. You're a man, so be manly. Communicate and share your emotions but remain strong, be dependable, make decisions, lead. If you want a bosom to cry on – that's what your mother's for, not your girlfriend.

# Wear condoms

You might as well get used to them early because there are more diseases out there jockeying for your Johnson than at any time in history.

# Aftershave . . .

. . . is for swarthy Europeans and guys who wear gold jewellery. Use it judiciously.

# Notice detail

An unfilled glass at a party, a new hairstyle, a certain angle of penetration. Women love it when you remember the little things.

# Brush your tongue

Those knobby bits at the rear of your tongue – better known as tastebuds – are a sponge for rancid smells. Give 'em a scrub every day – you don't wanna be the stinky-breath guy.

# Read the newspapers

There's nothing quite as scary as people whose sum knowledge of the world is what their parents have heard on talkback radio.

# Love foreplay

There's a lot more to lovemaking than thrashing about like a frog in a sock. Learn the art of foreplay and you'll join a sought-after club of men who are as concerned about their partner's pleasure as their own.

# Don't buy a leather couch

Resist the urge. It will pass, just like the desire to get that THUGLIFE tattoo on your stomach.

# Don't hold grudges

You're the one who suffers – the other person is happily getting on with their life.

# Drive a Volvo

Until you're at least twenty-five, by which time you should be out of the woods when it comes to doing stupid things in motor vehicles. Until then I want you safe in the old Swedish shock absorber.

# Things you will regret doing

- Hitting a woman
- Letting down your friends
- Not protecting your sister
- Running over a dog in a car

# Learn to play a musical instrument

It's far more mesmerising to the opposite sex than being able to play squash.

# Don't get a perm

Do I have to explain this?

# Don't share banknotes snorting coke

The blood vessels in your nose can rupture doing any drug nasally. That twenty-dollar note may be buying you a lifelong case of hepatitis.

# Don't smoke hydro

Hydroponic marijuana is full of fertilisers and pesticides. If you're going to have the odd joint, stick with naturally grown weed – and stop when the voices start.

# Never inject anything

It's so beyond crazy. You're breaking the sacred seal protecting you against the world – your skin.

# Trim your pubes

A neat bush is cleaner, sexier and makes your penis look bigger. Win–win if you ask me.

# Play a team sport

You'll get to know a lot of different guys, get plenty of back-up in street fights and have an end-of-season trip to look forward to. It will also teach you discipline and humility; big heads get brought down to earth quickly with twenty other men around.

# Never lose your temper

Is there a sadder sight than a grown man screaming and stamping his feet like a two-year-old because he's missed a flight or his steak's overcooked?

Don't be that guy.

# Don't lie to your mates

They will never forget it.

# Don't buy cheap shoes

They don't have to be Prada, just don't be getting about in a pair of Grosbys from Kmart. Shop with a woman who knows what she's doing and breathe deeply when it's time to pay.

# Never wear sandals

Ever. Never jog in Speedos. Ever.

# Learn to dance

If you have rhythm, use it. If not, get lessons. There's nothing more appealing than a guy who can sex it up on the dance floor while the other gumps are getting drunk enough to move their feet from side to side.

# Do the things during a relationship . . .

. . . you did at the beginning. Like getting her a drink when she's exhausted or leaving a flower on her dashboard because she's a wonderful person.

# Don't wax your chest

Or your legs or arms. Unless you're an Olympic swimmer. Or a ballet dancer. Then I'll understand. Somehow.

# Don't say things you'll regret during a break-up

I know it feels good to twist the knife during the final moments of a relationship, but trust me, when it's long finished you'll be proud you maintained your dignity.

# Start golfing early

It's a lame game, but it's all you'll have to do when you're sixty-five. You want geeky accountants lording it over you?

# Don't push in at the bar

You know damn well who was there first.

# Things you'll never regret doing

- Visiting your grandmother
- Standing up to a bully
- Skydiving
- Living in Paris
- Falling madly in love

# Don't wait for life to happen

Go on surfing adventures, drink absurd martinis, build a boat. The only difference between people involved in exciting stuff and everyone else is they go out and do it.

# Keep your word

Otherwise it devalues quickly.

TO MY DASHING SON . . .

# Ten per cent of people . . .

. . . will not like you no matter what you do. They just hate your head for some reason. Accept it. Move on.

# Be a gentleman

Which is defined as a man who makes others feel comfortable. People don't forget these things. Be nice to everyone, not just the ones who can advance you. You can make a lonely person's day just by having a joke with them at the bus stop.

# You don't have to be a great man

Just be a good man.

Lastly, to both
of you . . .

# Choose your reaction

If you learn one thing from this book, let it be this: no matter what somebody does to you or what life throws up, you can choose your response. Jesus called it turning the other cheek, Buddhists practise it by reacting to good and bad with equanimity, and the ancient Jews saw it as a case of never laying blame on others for the way you feel.

Blame is epidemic nowadays, but you need to understand it's as pointless as getting angry about the weather. In this life, you control nothing but yourself. If you can overcome your impulse to blame and choose your reaction instead of doing what feels 'natural', a magnificent life presents itself where you are master of every decision you make.

Controlling impulse, whether it's the desire to hate, hit the bottle or have a second helping, is the hardest test in life, but ultimately, my darling children, it will set you free.

PENGUIN BOOKS

Published by the Penguin Group
Penguin Group (Australia)
707 Collins Street, Melbourne, Victoria 3008, Australia
(a division of Pearson Australia Group Pty Ltd)
Penguin Group (USA) Inc.
375 Hudson Street, New York, New York 10014, USA
Penguin Group (Canada)
90 Eglinton Avenue East, Suite 700, Toronto, Canada ON M4P 2Y3
(a division of Pearson Penguin Canada Inc.)
Penguin Books Ltd
80 Strand, London WC2R 0RL England
Penguin Ireland
25 St Stephen's Green, Dublin 2, Ireland
(a division of Penguin Books Ltd)
Penguin Books India Pvt Ltd
11 Community Centre, Panchsheel Park, New Delhi – 110 017, India
Penguin Group (NZ)
67 Apollo Drive, Rosedale, North Shore 0632, New Zealand
(a division of Pearson New Zealand Ltd)
Penguin Books (South Africa) (Pty) Ltd
Rosebank Office Park, Block D, 181 Jan Smuts Avenue, Parktown North, Johannesburg 2196, South Africa

Penguin Books Ltd, Registered Offices: 80 Strand, London, WC2R 0RL, England

First published by Penguin Group (Australia), 2006

15 17 19 20 18 16 14



Design by Nikki Townsend and Patrick Leong © Penguin Group (Australia)

Cover photograph by photolibrary

Typeset in Bernhard Modern by Post Pre-press Group, Brisbane, Queensland
Printed and bound in China by Everbest Printing Co. Ltd.

National Library of Australia
Cataloguing-in-Publication data:

Brito, Sam de.

No tattoos before you're thirty.

ISBN 978 0 14 300417 2.

1. Australian wit and humor. 2. Life skills - Humor. I. Title.

A827.4

penguin.com.au